*Commissioned by the Royal Liverpool Philharmonic Society
and re-dedicated to the memory of
George Szell*

SYMPHONY NO. 2

WILLIAM WALTON

MOVEMENTS

Allegro molto	p. 1
Lento assai	p. 81
Passacaglia: Theme, Variations, Fugato, and Coda-Scherzando	p. 114

Music Department
OXFORD UNIVERSITY PRESS
Oxford and New York

ORCHESTRATION

2 Flutes
Piccolo (doubling Flute III)
2 Oboes
Cor Anglais (doubling Oboe III)
2 Clarinets (second doubling Clarinet in E flat)
Bass Clarinet (doubling Clarinet III)
3 Bassoons (third doubling Contra Bassoon)
4 Horns
3 Trumpets
3 Trombones
Tuba
Timpani
Percussion (4 players): Tamb. Mil., Caisse Claire, Piatti, Gran Cassa, Glock., Vibra., Xylo., Tamburino, Bell in D
Piano
Celeste
2 Harps
Strings

NOTES

This work was commissioned by the Royal Liverpool Philharmonic Society and was given its first performance by the Royal Liverpool Philharmonic Orchestra, conducted by John Pritchard, on 2 September 1960, as part of the Edinburgh International Festival.

Duration 27 minutes ($8\frac{1}{2}$-$9\frac{1}{2}$-9)

It is recorded on CBS 61087 by the Cleveland Orchestra under George Szell.

Large-size scores and orchestral parts are available on hire from the publishers.

I

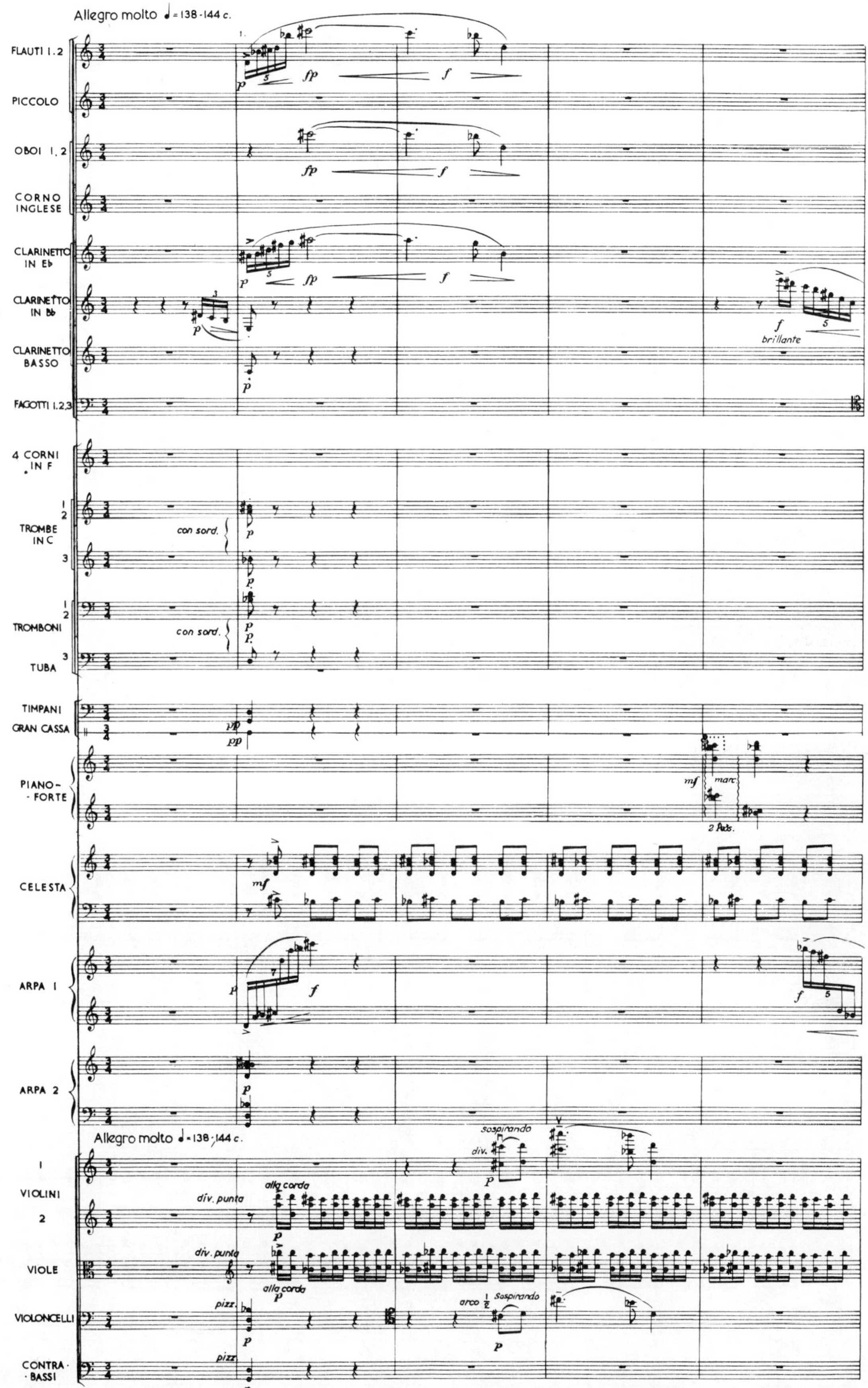

OXFORD UNIVERSITY PRESS, MUSIC DEPARTMENT, WALTON STREET, OXFORD OX2 6DP

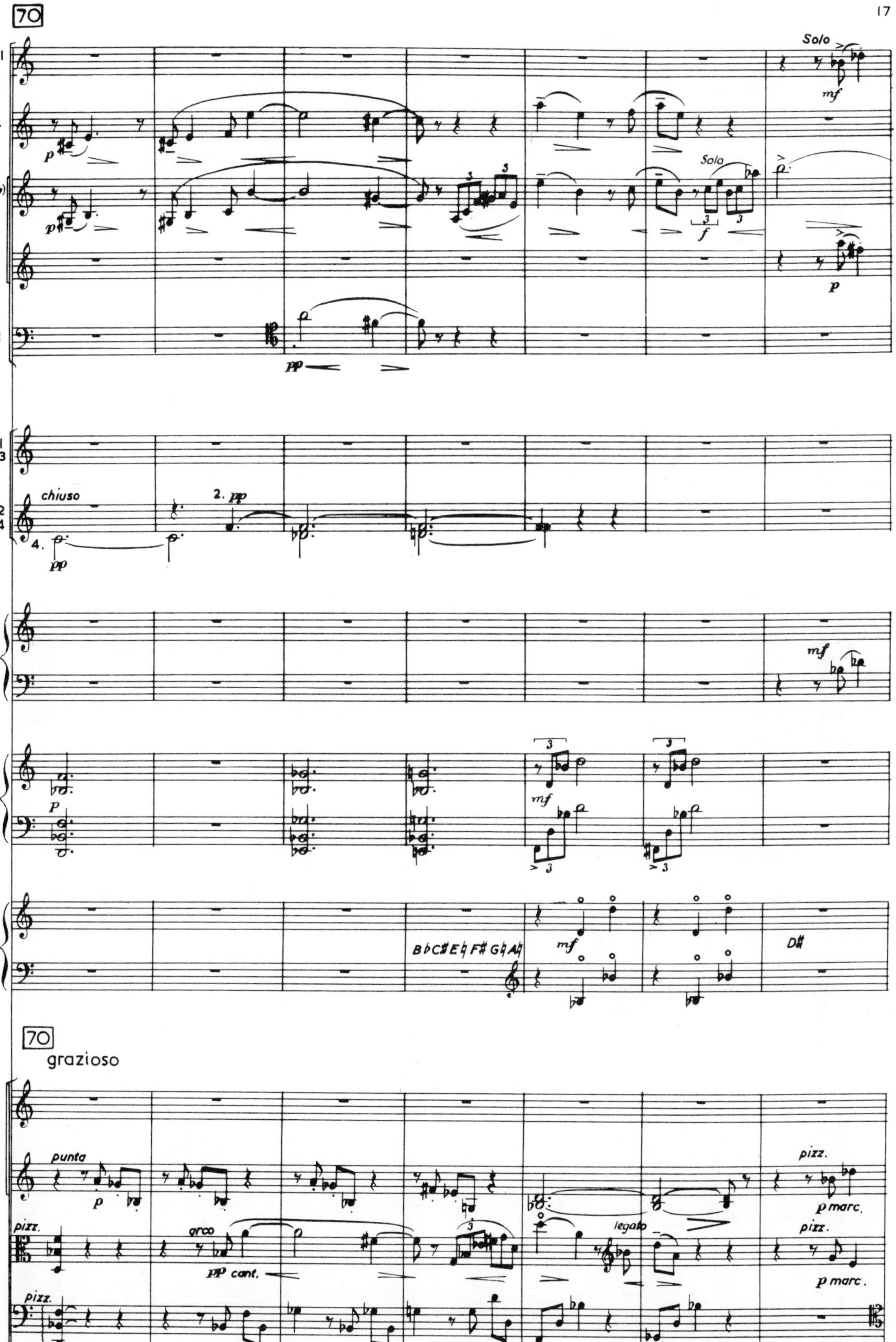
70
Fl. I
Solo
mf
C.i.
p
Cl.(B♭)
p
Solo
f
Cl. b.
p
Fg. I
pp
1
3
Cor. (F)
2
4
chiuso
4.
pp
2. pp
Cel.
mf
Arpa I
p
mf
Arpa 2
B♭C♯E♮F♯G♮A♮
mf
D♯
70
grazioso
I
Vl.
2
punta
p
pizz.
p marc.
Vle.
pizz.
arco
pp cant.
legato
pizz.
p marc.
Vlc.
pizz.
pp
Cb.
pizz. SOLO
pp

22

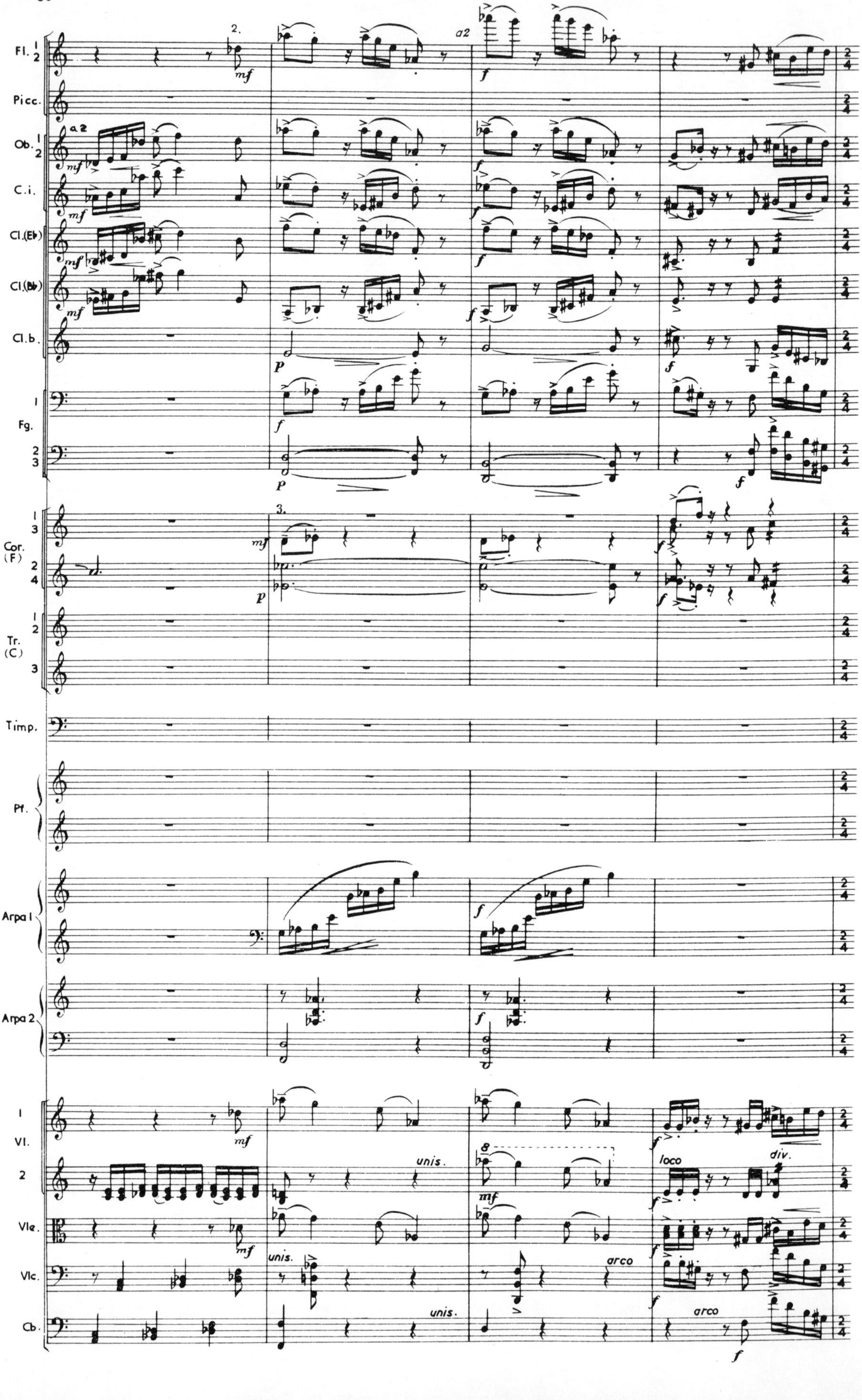
Fl. 1 2
Picc.
Ob. 1 2
C.i.
Cl.(Eb)
Cl.(Bb)
Cl.b.
Fg. 1 2 3
Cor. (F) 1 3 2 4
Tr. (C) 1 2 3
Timp.
Pf.
Arpa I
Arpa 2
Vl. 1 2
Vle.
Vlc.
Cb.
2.
a2
3.
unis.
arco
loco
div.

45

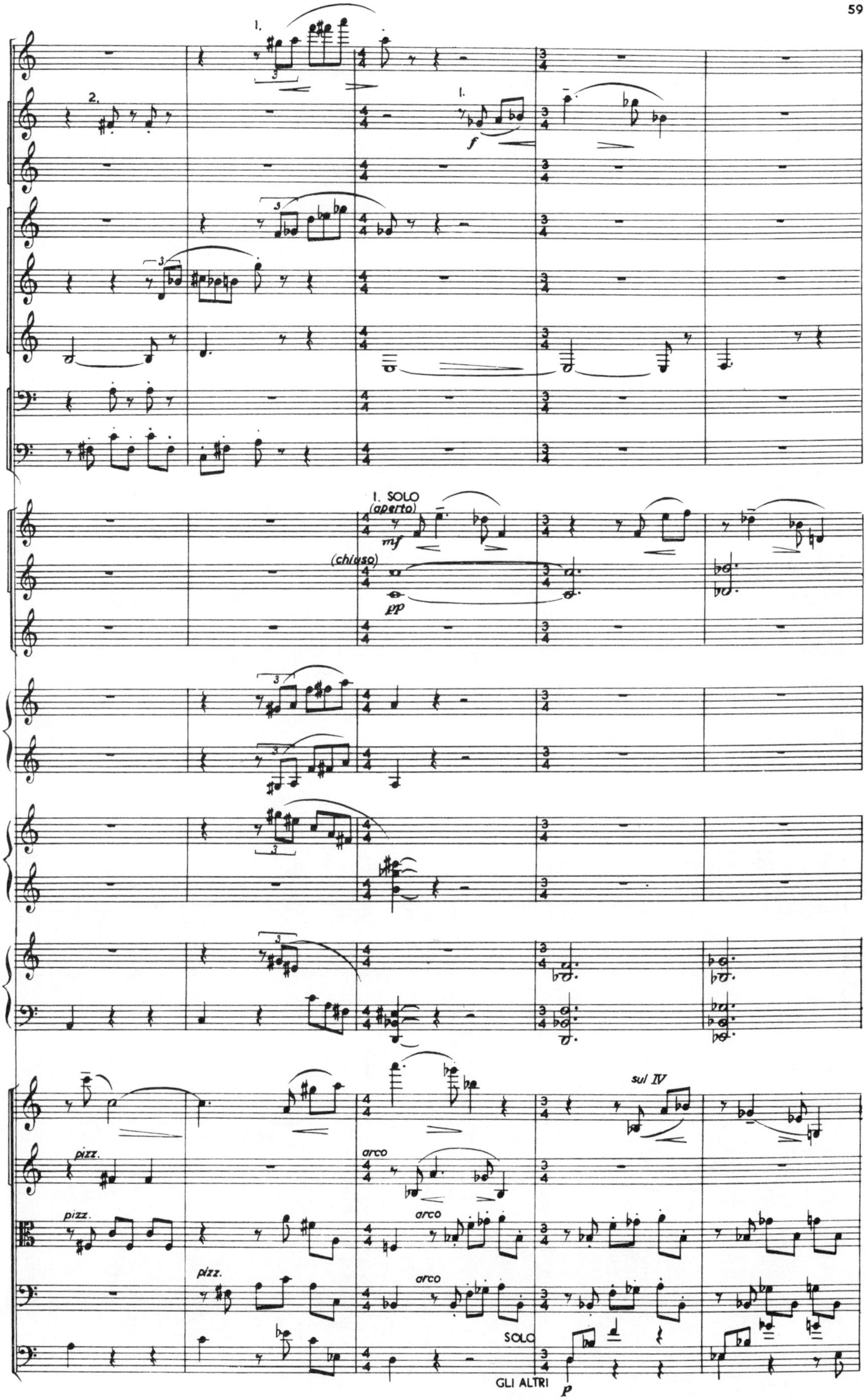
1.
2.
1.
f
1. SOLO
(aperto)
mf
(chiuso)
pp
pizz.
arco
sul IV
SOLO
GLI ALTRI
p

80

II

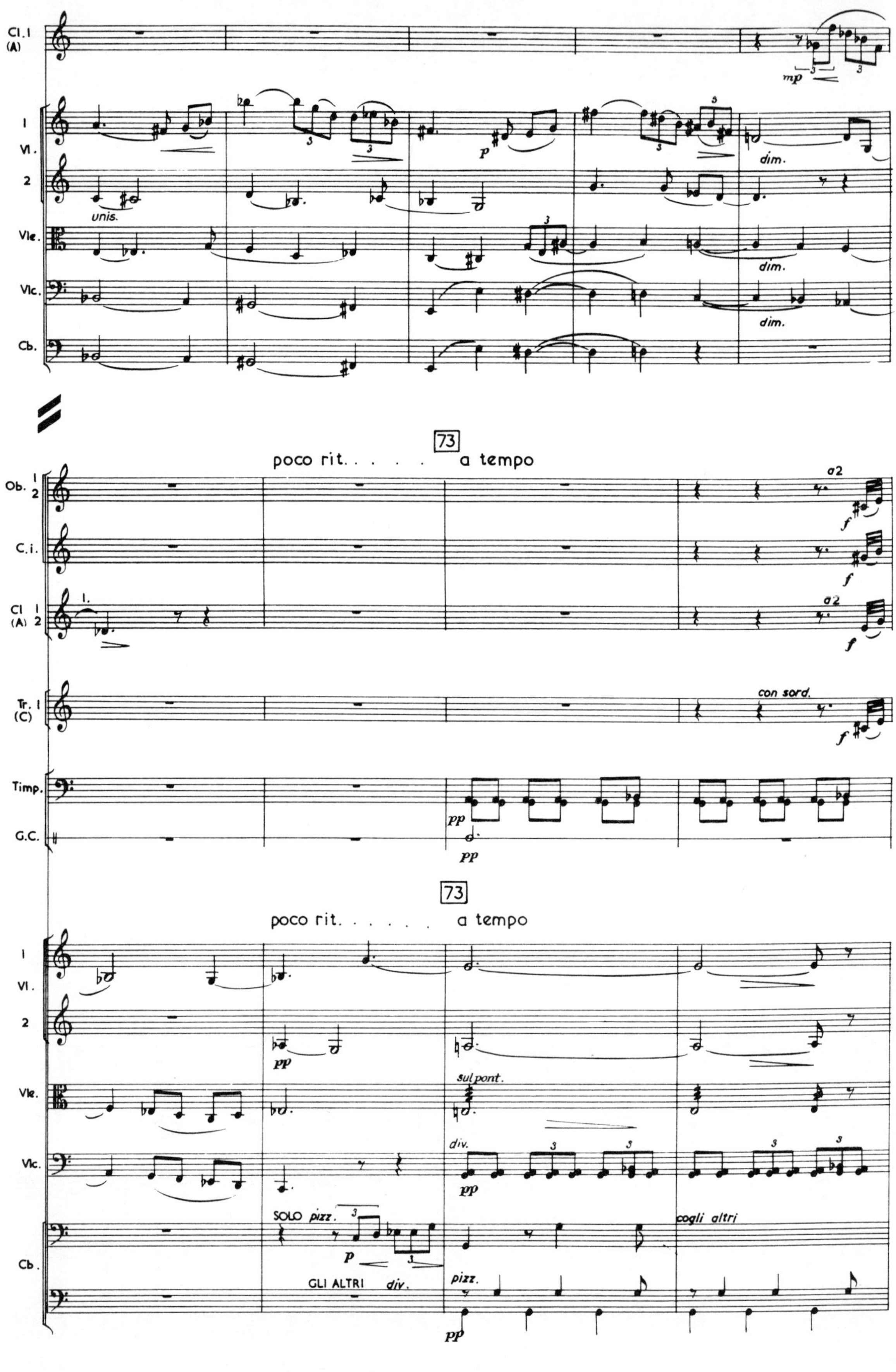
Cl. I (A)
Vl. 1
Vl. 2
Vle.
Vlc.
Cb.
mp
p
dim.
unis.
73
poco rit. . . . . . a tempo
Ob. 1 2
C. i.
Cl 1 2 (A)
Tr. I (C)
Timp.
G.C.
a2
1.
con sord.
f
pp
sul pont.
div.
SOLO pizz.
coglі altri
GLI ALTRI div.
pizz.

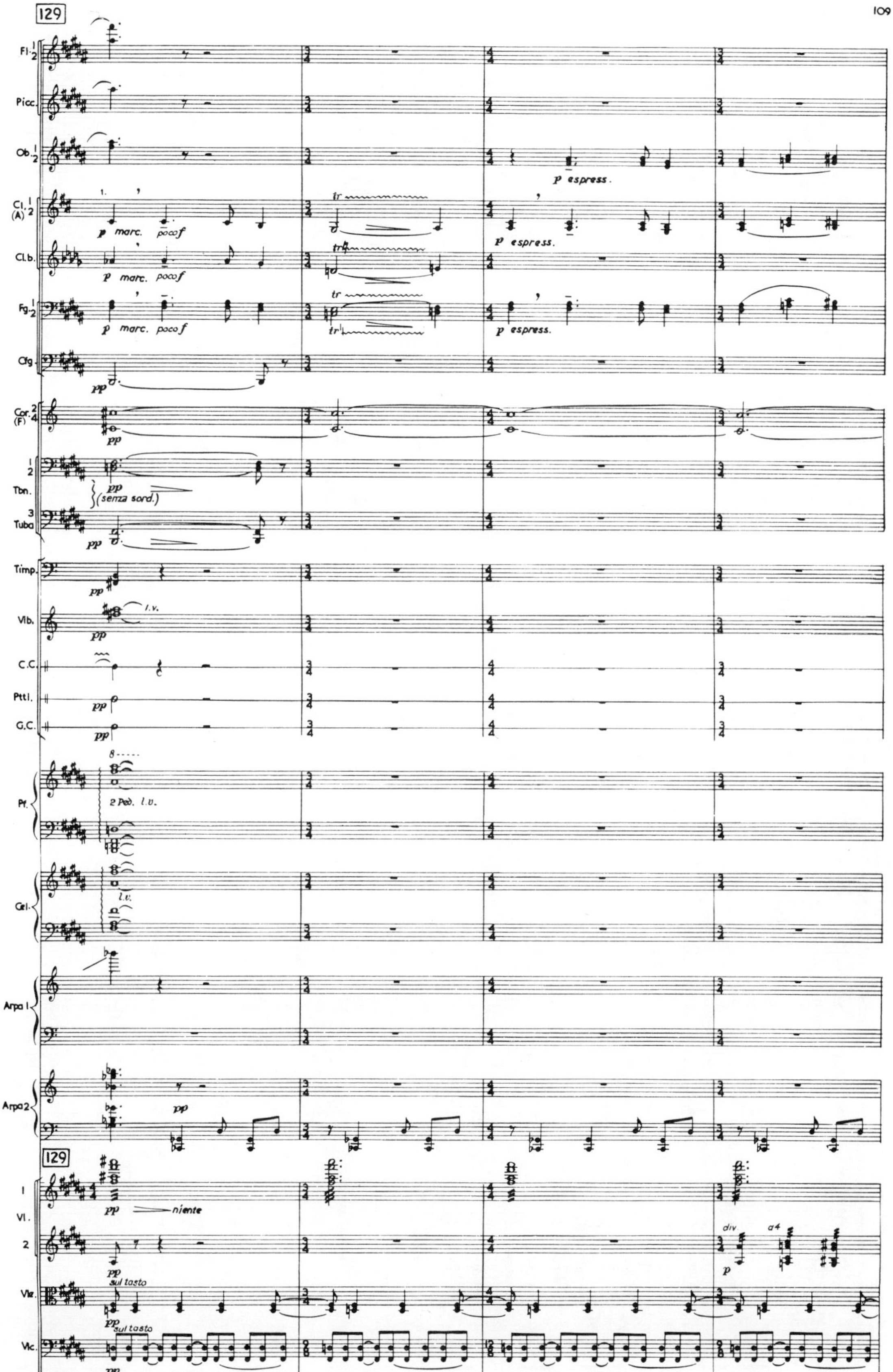
129
Fl. 1 2
Picc.
Ob. 1 2
Cl. 1 2 (A)
Cl.b.
Fg. 1 2
Cfg.
Cor. 2 4 (F)
Tbn. 1 2
3 Tuba
Timp.
Vib.
C.C.
Pttl.
G.C.
Pf.
Cel.
Arpa 1
Arpa 2
129
Vl. 1
2
Vle.
Vlc.
Cb.
p marc. poco f
p espress.
tr
pp
(senza sord.)
l.v.
2 Ped. l.v.
pp
niente
div
a4
p
sul tasto
unis.

III

PASSACAGLIA
Tema - Risoluto (♩ = 112 c.)

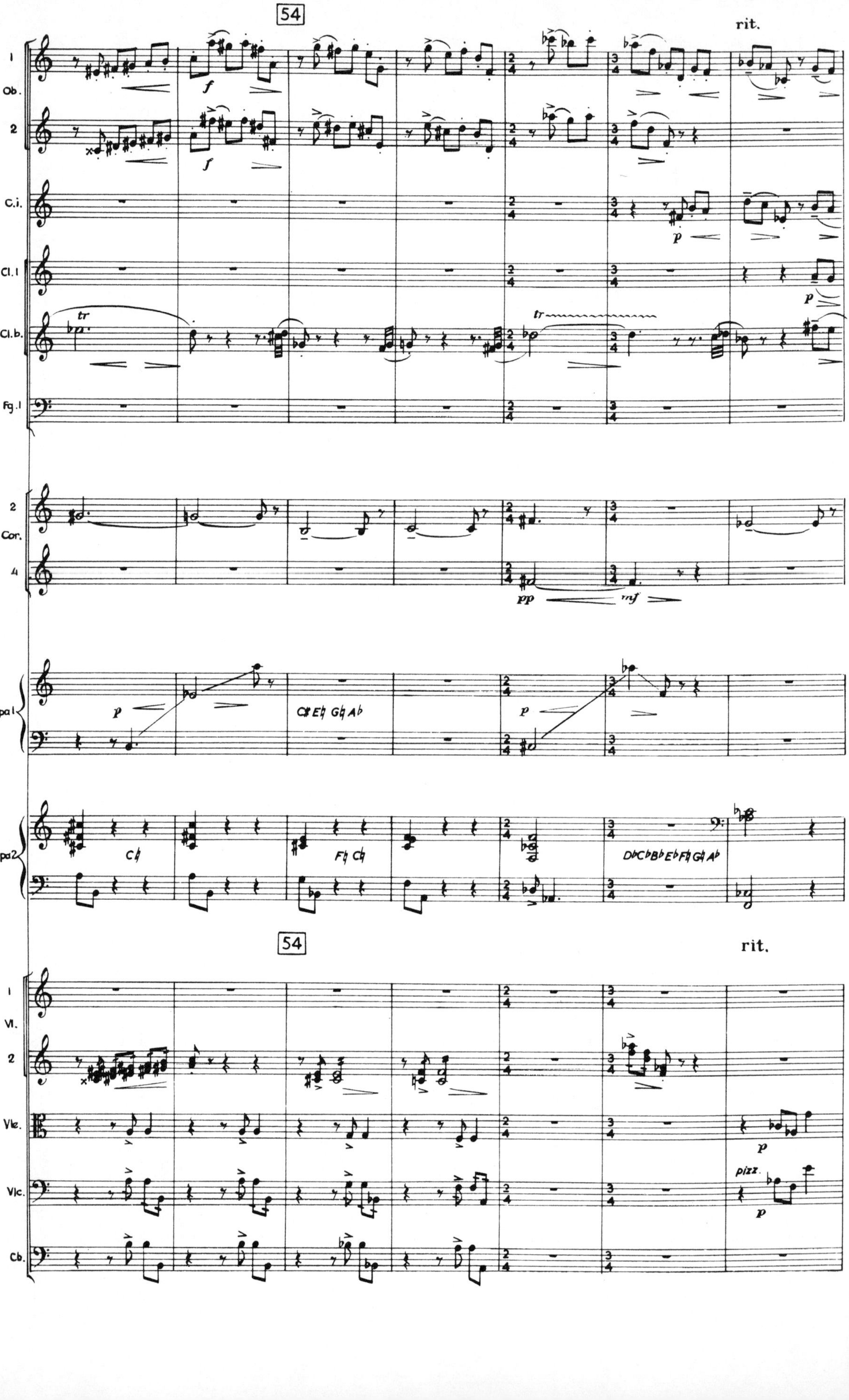
54
rit.
Ob.
C.i.
Cl.1
Cl.b.
Fg.1
Cor.
Arpa1
C♯E♮ G♮A♭
Arpa2
C♮
F♮ C♮
D♭C♭B♭E♭F♮G♮A♭
54
rit.
Vl.
Vle.
Vlc.
pizz.
Cb.

102 Var. 7. Impetuoso ♩ = 138-144